First published in Great Britain in 2001 by
POETRY NOW
Remus House,
Coltsfoot Drive,
Peterborough, PE2 9JX
Telephone (01733) 898101
Fax (01733) 313524

Copyright Contributors 2001

HB ISBN 0 75432 666 7
SB ISBN 0 75432 667 5

FOREWORD

Although we are a nation of poets we are accused of not reading poetry, or buying poetry books. After many years of listening to the incessant gripes of poetry publishers, I can only assume that the books they publish, in general, are books that most people do not want to read.

Poetry should not be obscure, introverted, and as cryptic as a crossword puzzle: it is the poet's duty to reach out and embrace the world.

The world owes the poet nothing and we should not be expected to dig and delve into a rambling discourse searching for some inner meaning.

The reason we write poetry (and almost all of us do) is because we want to communicate: an ideal; an idea; or a specific feeling. Poetry is as essential in communication, as a letter; a radio; a telephone, and the main criterion for selecting the poems in this anthology is very simple: they communicate.

ARE THE STARS STILL SHINING?

Edited by

Rebecca Mee

CONTENTS

MILLENNIUM STADIUM
(Heart of the Country)

From white skeletal bones
hangs flesh;
heart beats intermittently;
blood roars,
subsides.

Mirrored in Taff's sides,
recollections.
In soft, rippled faces
lamp-lights
trace pouring crowds,
Taff's tongue licks banks;
ground
sounds drum of dancing feet.

As night clears,
lamp-light eyes close,
city's pores open -
snores.

Marc Harris

WORLD IN AN EGGSHELL

Have you ever noticed the twilight hours:
The setting of the sun?
The flavours in the sunset?
The anguish that begun?
The working of the labour?
The lowered rope that grows?
Comes the morning promise
Of another day of woe
Have you seen my child
Before the break of dawn?
Have you heard him labour
As he breathes through your lungs worn?
Have you turned the key yet
Before the sodium glow?
Have you had a thought yet
As to where you want to go?
Will you dream of daybreak
Or is your heart too slow?
Put the ransom in your pocket
You don't need to say hello
But one day I will meet you
And thank you for it all
The life you spent denying
That you caused
One single hole.

Anora Kay

ENEMY ACTION

Presently we are concerned
about a woman named Rose.
She, one of those many,
had told us this was her name
when we had responded earlier
to her calling, but it is a while now
since her voice has been heard
again.

Our urgent concern for Rose increases
as time passes. Soon now the site
needs must be cleared.

Stricken somewhere amongst debris
from which she will not rise alive,
stilly she lies.

Her husband has come, to mourn
Unrisen Rose.

Louise Rogers

ENDOWMENT

Lost, alone and quite forsaken
I feel I've found the end to life
All I held precious is taken
Now misery has become rife.

This is more than a rut I am stuck in
Much more than an abyss of woe
Where totally nothing is working
And only pain and self pity flow.

Here the heart of hell engulfs you
And takes you as one of their own
Sure it's the way, I know this is true
For I can only curse, moan and groan.

A middle-aged man with potential
Who's gone and got hopelessly lost
Who now finds it almost essential
To struggle and repay the cost.

Hugh S McKay

LESSONS IN LIFE

Big girls don't cry
But at four
I am too young to know
The wisdom of swallowing tears
So it is with Christmas Day anticipation
That I hear footsteps on the landing
Bringing you to me
Finally you stand
Framed in the doorway
And there you are still . . .
Then a sudden twitch
As covers are pulled down
And stinging blows are delivered
By the belt
Normally used to hold yourself together
There is no pain as the final cut
Severs the cord
Which made me yours
Across the divide that grows between
Knowledge arrives unfashionably early
Eager to spread the news
That I am truly alone

Deborah Davis

EUSTACIA'S HEATH

('Her presence brought memories of Bourbon roses, rubies
tropical midnights' - Thomas Hardy - 'The Return of the Native')

And you sit and watch your sand run out,
With fragile dreams of faded grandeur.

With your hair like ebony evenings,
Your eyes blindly searching far and wide.
Your hollow rooms sigh with your solitude
And their dark corners offer no place to hide.

Gluttonous freedom,
Starved suffering.
A prison without bars
And secrets,
Too many secrets
And so little time.

It's not your fault the lovers love without love,
That you had a map to infinity and never found it.
It's not the fantastic flame's fault,
If the maddened moths must dance around it.

And you're desperate to remember the scent
Of your shattered glass roses.
They whisper cruelly with wonder,
And say nothing at all.
He built you a pedestal to a soft, safe heaven,
Do you expect him to catch you when you finally fall?

You will fall through his insecure promises, lost goddess,
And the fat black night and its blood will choke you.
And what an irony that you asked it to come,
And stain all the good you've ever done!
And what a tragedy that it could never tame you,
Wild lover!

Your silent serenity scratches his thin soul,
He sees his future and it hasn't happened yet,
And though your compassion lets him forgive,
Your passion will never let him forget,
And never have you looked more beautiful
Burning fire child,
As you do now in docile death.

Lorna Meehan

BETRAYAL

Black pupils, darker than coal
Softer and more luxurious than silk,
Your skin.
If you were to embrace me,
I would collapse like a pyramid of cards.
The loving dedicated will that built me
Would vanish in the falling.
The point from which I can not return,
The mystery of the black hole gravity that pulls me,
What lies beyond?
Deep down I know,
My conscience is shackled.
I focus on the moment,
Not the stab from a blunted knife,
Thrust into the back of my faithful wife.

Paul Willis

REPORTER SAYS,
'NOTHING'S GOING TO CHANGE TILL WE DO'

She was proud of her yellow hair,
And prouder still, when he, the debonair
Came courting her.
They loved and lived in that village by the border there.
They took him out; shot him before her eyes.

I saw her standing in the hopeless line,
Clutching their yellow haired babe.
Her lovely hair careless in the wind,
And no light in her eyes.

Could I have said that dying does not lead to death?
Could I have smoothed her brow, removed her tears?
Could I be healer, she the sufferer?
Would not that a separation make?

Too late to say, there is no you or me; there's only us,
It isn't your hurt or mine but ours.
That even in the worst is the heart and soul of God.
That only good can lead to peace.
Too late to say, in love there is no war, too late . . . words separate,
While such fury hurled its hatred, hate on hate.

For on the day that evil stormed that peaceful place
I knew there was only one thing I could do,
Begin to change the me and start anew.

Margaret Gill

SOUNDS WRONG

What an orator!
A latter-day Churchill
    Sangster
    Luther-King even
Little wonder that they
Invited me.

And yet
Five minutes into the talk
They turn away distracted
    restless
    edgy even.

I crack a joke
To illustrate a point.

Momentarily their attention is recalled
A buzz stirs through the crowd
Collective smirks.

And then, as one man
Again, distraction
But by what?

Yet, that sound?
It comes from over there

It is . . . it is . . .
(it can't be!)
But it is . . .
The announcement of the winner of the . . .
National Lottery!

Dishevelled
They shove off home.

Perhaps next week?

The baby has been thrown out
With the bath water!

J C Crowe

No Win

Never have his dinner ready
You're getting at him for being late.
Make sure his dinner is on the table
After a hard day he won't want to wait.

Keep the children up for him
So they won't forget their father.
For God's sake can't you get them in bed?
I'm too tired for their noise and bother.

What's with the sexy underwear?
Wasting my money, looking silly.
Can't you wear something sexier in bed?
Pyjamas are such a passion killer.

Never initiate sex
He'll tell you when he wants it.
Don't turn away and go to sleep
Freezing me out, you frigid bitch.

When he hits you, don't fight back
It just makes the problem grow.
Never, ever cower away
His guilt will make him hit you more.

Just follow the rules
And you'll never be abused.
Unless of course
You ask for it . . .

Grace Green

WHAT WILL IT TAKE?

What price peace for the world?
How much blood must be shed?
Before man opens his eyes to reality,
and we can cease to count the dead.
How many lives must be wasted?
How many families torn apart?
Before man looks deep inside of him,
and sees the love inside his heart.
How blind can mankind be?
What tragedy will it take?
To make us understand the destruction,
and put right our mistake.
To cast aside the weapons,
and reach for the enemy's out-stretched hand.
To begin to live in friendship,
as our creator planned.

M A Challis

IN MY DREAM

In my dream I saw all the angels in heaven
Looking just as I imagined they would
With the saviour, 'the Lord Jesus Christ'
In the midst of them all, there He stood!
I could clearly see he was crying
No longer did he look steadfast and strong
Hurting from the scene he looked down on
At all, throughout mankind, that is wrong
He sees a world where compassion's on ration
Where hate and violence now rules the day
He sees all that's good and decent destroyed
While rogues all around, have their way
Man's inhumanity to man has saddened His heart
Yet He knows this will change given time
And those who upset the rhythm of life
Will, one day, pay for their crime!

Karl Jakobsen

THEN WE WERE ONE

It is true what they say
'No one knows what the loss of a loved one can mean
Until it happens to you'.
As we go along life's pathway
In good times and sad, on each other we lean
Love keeping us strong in all we do.

As I walk down Memory Lane
I look at others, in their eyes
To see if they feel like me.
Sometimes see the grief and pain
As on they walk as if in a dream, wondering why,
Wondering why it has to be.

Yes, there are so many like us.
The thought giving strength in life to battle on
And help through each phase.
In the Lord we put our trust
And seek His guiding hand to rest upon
To help through empty days.

It's good to have a friend good and true
With whom to mull things over and bare the soul.
Helps to lift the cloud from our eyes.
It helps to get another view
As we travel on to reach our goal
And be with loved ones in the skies.

But enough of this sorrow.
Life is for living and enjoying to the full.
Pleasure from it let us derive.
Let us give thanks for the morrow
Give thanks for all things bright and beautiful
And give thanks for being alive.

Tess Walton

In The Culling Fields Of Cumbria

Think of the May blossom, gosh! It is spring,
Spring is the time for new birth it brings.
In fields young lambs go jumping and skipping,
Hedgerows of primroses, thro' bluebells go tripping.
Think of the meadows of rich grasses with plover,
Young calves at play and cows in the clover,
In the culling fields of Cumbria.

Imagine the fields and fells without sheep,
No cows in the barn, on hay used to sleep.
We cannot imagine how farmers feel,
Proud men and women, hearts not made of steel.
He checks the cow herd, strolls through the barn,
Vet's been around they came to no harm.
Still hope against hope, they will not go away,
To the culling fields of Cumbria.

The farmer heard tell, some distance beyond,
A neighbour's cattle and sheep lay dead on the ground.
The dreaded news, afraid now and fear,
If that wind should carry, now see a tear.
Oh, please don't let it be so . . . pray,
Don't let them take all his life's work away.
Just think of it, it is really spring,
In the culling fields of Cumbria.

For business in Cumbria, they say we are open,
To an art exhibition we went hoping,
Yes, it is spring for we hear the birds sing
Hedgerows of daffodils, joy they do bring.
As we top the brow, the Pennines we view,
Snow-capped they glisten, shine all anew,
Across the culling fields of Cumbria.

But soon see black smoke rising high,
And we turn away, as we give a big sigh.
There are signs the tractors have been this way
And a smell in the nostrils of all this decay,
An eerie feeling as we pass empty fields,
Farms empty, quietness where once it did yield
Now in the culling fields of Cumbria.

Thin smoke still rises from newly laid ground,
Where all those poor animals now make no sound,
A quiet stillness creeps o'er the land
Horrible feelings, sweating, sweating of hands,
Smoke still rises from east and to west,
As we turn for home, it is a hard test
For farmers and businesses, no feelings of spring now,
In the culling fields of Cumbria.

Irene Lee

THE FIRST GOOD SAMARITAN

Ribs like forks
Cutting through the falsehood of our dreams
To blank begging eyes
Bulging out of half-made doll frames
Half-made bones
To love our neighbour part-time
Like a 'Tiny Tears'
As we practise motherhood
To a distant relative
A third world
Or another planet
It might as well be.

Why?
Who is going to pick up the broken china
A poor substitute for our broken teapot
They don't give us tea bags
As they lie there dying
As if it were second nature.

Like a quiet note
It hasn't registered
They are outside our Garden of Eden
In their own wasteland
Who will be the first Good Samaritan?

Claire Booth

GOOD AND EVIL

You ask why there's so much injustice in the world
Look around, it's those who are in the world
That cause such suffering, such pain
These people are quite insane
They're to blame.

Some say they're not insane
They're totally evil
What is the difference I tell you to ask
Believe me it's a jolly hard task!

None of us know
What the other is thinking
But at the end of the day
All I can say

Is if you believe in God
Follow the Lord
Do only good
You won't go far wrong
And God will give you a gift
And that is to be strong.

T Hartley

FOR HEAVEN'S SAKE

I'm from Northern Ireland and I want peace
I pray each night that the troubles will cease
From bombings and shootings please set me free
Stabbings and beatings there's hundreds like me
I hear about these and it causes me pain
Unfortunately tomorrow it's more of the same
Discrimination, intimidation when will it end
If you're not one of us we won't call you friend
If you fly the Tricolour or Union Jack
For heaven's sake, cut us some slack
Now we must live together side by side
And fight to stop this evil tide
That sweeps across our lovely land
Pushed on by men with gun in hand.

Paul O'Boyle

2051

No end to insanity
Of the five letter word
Diamonds for guns
Gold for teeth
Money for drugs

Poor live on empty
Pockets full of love
On this fine tuned engine
Ready to explode
Run out of juice
Simply implode

Air full of smog
Dark brown instead of green
No birds or fish
Just animals breed for
The humans' machine

Where humans fight nature
In the longest of wars
Only we keep that score.

Nigel Thomson

INTOLERANCE

Intolerance, a human curse!
The greatest one by far,
For those who are intolerant,
Don't seem to know they are,
How many people teach their young,
All humans are our kin?
Then fault a stranger for their tongue,
Or judge them by their skin,
If deafness was our common plight,
You'd sound the same as me,
If something robbed you of your sight,
What colour would I be?
How can we boast about and praise
Our breed and land of birth,
We're members of the human race,
Our birthplace is the earth.

M L Burns

IF I WERE A MILLIONAIRE

If I were a millionaire
I could show just how much I care
I cold clean up the rivers
I could clean up the seas
I'd replant the meadows
I'd replant the trees
The world it would be
Such a much better place
If I were a millionaire.

Greeny 2001

MURDER IN OUR MIDST

Why is it such a violent life?
So many people in such strife.
Why do we hate instead of love?

We read in the paper here today,
The children cannot go out to play.
Murder was committed down in the wood,
Although the victim fought all they could.
Now we are all living in fear,
Especially the ones who live so near.

Could it be one of the village folk,
We are all so numb, it is no joke.
We fear to tread outside our doors,
We cannot walk across the moors.

With windows and doors tightly shut,
To neighbours we hardly speak, but
Until this criminal is caught,
Our lives will be so very fraught.
For everyone is a suspect here,
That is why we live in fear.

Why is it such a violent life?
Why do we not love instead of fight?

Barbara Stanczyszyn

BLIND ALLEYS

Blind alleys collide
And brick walls stand tall
Thus Stormont begins
To crumble and fall

Guns that were silent
Are heard now to stir
Because politicians
Still cannot concur

A dark day is dawning
Its daggers are out
So hungry the blades
That have been sent to scout

A vastness of terror
A bottomless pit
Where those who must suffer
At politics spit

Blind alleys collide
And the brick walls remain
The structure of Stormont
Falls under the strain

A vision of peace
And the promise of calm
Begins its regression
To war, fear and harm.

Kim Montia

LONE PERSON'S DILEMMA

Hospitals were meant for the sick
    Not anymore
If you get admitted
There's always an eye on the door

For elderly people
    Those on their own
Illness doesn't count
It's the Nursing Home

All the pen-pushers
    Waving a stick
One has plenty to cope with
If they are sick

Have you a house
    Property to sell
To pay for your treatment
If unwell

They worked so hard
    To pay their way
Now Big Brother comes
To take it away

Those very ill
    Can suffer the most
Some are pushed
From pillar to post

They thought the Health Service
    Would come to their aid
Most worked hard
Contributions paid

It's the old and the feeble
    We must worry about
Because they are too ill
To grumble and shout

The National Health Service
    Has treated most of us well
It's the few in great need
That have a story to tell

I've had my say
It's out of my head
Should I get old
And decrepit

Perhaps I won't need
    A hospital bed
For the convenient way to go
Is just to drop dead.

Gladys C'Ailceta

PEACE ON EARTH

Peace, we can't have peace,
What is peace?
Is it love
That we find on the wings
Of a dove?
Does it come,
Handed on a plate
For us to grab
Before it's ate?
Is it early to bed - or night
Before it's too late.
To breathe is to live
And to live is to die
That's the injustice of earth
As it passes us by
And we not knowing why.

Dorothy Rowe

LOVE IS GOOD FOR LOVING

The sky is good for flying, flying
But no birds are trailing the clouds
Aeroplanes ablaze are falling, falling.

The sea is good for sailing, sailing
But no persons are bathing in the sea
Ships with loads of men are sinking, sinking.

The Earth is good for sharing, sharing
But the hearth is empty, women alone,
Men of flesh and bone, sent by hearts of stone are dying, dying.

Love is good for loving, loving
But the sky, the sea and the Earth are empty
And love is crying, crying.

Angela Matheson

LOST CHILDHOOD

The child's face fills with pain
crying and lonely hurt yet again
They look to the future and hope
but in reality where is the scope?

The parent's hurt is just the same
until hurting the child becomes a dangerous game
The sadness we see is all around
We would prefer to hear a different sound

Someone to listen
Someone to care
What happens to children
in these very sad years?

Julia I Bell

THOUGHTS

Governments can pass as many
laws as they like
yet they can't stop people thinking.

As long as that fountain of knowledge
runs clear
people can't be stopped from drinking.

Life seems to be like this today
not enough work - not enough pay.

And when will all wars
come to an end.

Can you tell me this my friend?

Audrey E Ritzkowski

In Memory Of Taglang

Taglang as a dirty little tramp tagged
Anywhere he stood beside you for a chat
A foul smell permeated the place
In his tattered trousers and faded jacket
With crumbs in his rag bag
For hours he could discourse on discipline and rules
Always gesticulating while highlighting these key issues
Once he set foot on the pedestrian crossing
A nearby car must stop
At unruly drivers he would shout
'Read your Highway Code.'

Overwhelmed with a deep-seated anger
While reflection on the society's downhill
So many lax and corrupt politicians
Turned him into a crosspatch
His vision for a humane and just society
Where peace and love must prevail over hatred and violence
Listen as long as you could stand the stink
Goodness, compassion, love, jolliness
In the face of the 62 year-old tramp flamed
Longing for a society of humane kindness
While remaining blind to his squalid-stricken conditions
Who could trust his honesty and fairness?

After a hospital treatment due to a malaise once
His house disinfected and foul furniture removed by sanitary services
He continued to overlook cleanliness
With always a layer of dirt over his face
In the bins for food he constantly hunted
Despite enough money from pension for a decent living.

Taglang chose to be a nonentity
His unhappy childhood and past poverty
To death dogged him.

At Amboise cemetery lies his body
No tombstone - wreath laid by nobody
Nearby rests a famous MP - drafter of the French constitution
Though her icy hands death lays on everybody
Self-destruction Taglang wrecked.

Dan Chellumben

THE FAMINE ISN'T ANY FAULT OF MINE

This famine isn't any fault of mine
It's the rebel who burns my maize
They sell cattle for many dollars
Then shoot guns in drunken rage.

This famine isn't any fault of mine
It's power-led groups to blame
Corrupt politicians are numerous
With values much the same.

The famine isn't any fault of mine
As bodies lie dead in the heat
I haven't strength to bury them
With so little food to eat.

Westerners have a conscience
They put shoulder to the wheel
Send essential goods and money
Which rebels promptly steal.

Alex Branthwaite

READ ALL ABOUT IT

Read all about it
Man stabbed to death in the street
Murderer on the loose
Read all about it
Read all about it
Boy killed in arson attack
Girl beaten black and blue
So many cases of violence
It's hardly something new

People's pain strung across the front page
Like we just won World War Two
Comments made
What a shame, so young to die
But no one really cares

No one hears or sees the victim's pain,
Just the news
It's just another story
Another day's news

No one sees the aftermath
The shattered family lives
No one sees the reality
That it could happen to them too.

Nicola Morley

WAR

As she cowers and hides
bombs explode on every side
Vacant eyes sad little face
don't you think it's a disgrace
what war does to this young child
is hidden deep inside
She watches loved ones hurt
or killed and even sees
their blood that is spilt
As a child she does not understand
the war that's ravaged her land
a sad young girl with sad sad eyes
with nothing left inside to let her cry
Why does this happen time and again
it's down to man to end this shame

Valerie Black

FOOT AND MOUTH

Fires are burning all over the land,
There's a stench of burnt flesh in the air.
Farmers are crying, bereft of their loss
And church bells ring out everywhere!

This Government says 'It's all sorted,
Don't you worry, we'll soon stamp it out!'
But the cases increase by the truckload,
Poor dumb creatures, all shot, without doubt'

And the bells still ring out in the churches
And the farmers are still sad and bereft;
As poor sheep and their lambs go to slaughter
It's a wonder there are any more left!

The bodies are piled high in the trenches
Of cattle that gave us milk, cheese and meat,
And men stand and gaze at the carnage,
And gag at the smell, sight and heat!

And *still* the bells ring out in mourning
For each animal killed every day,
Whilst those farmers whose livestock are still healthy,
Pray, that is how they will stay!

And I, like you, pray along with them
That this foot and mouth soon men will contain,
So that healthy lambs, sheep and cattle
Will graze in our fields once again!

Sylvia E L Reynolds

IS IT FAIR?

One of the earliest lessons we learn,
Is that life is not really fair.
We ought to try to balance this rule
By showing each other we care.

It isn't fair that people are ill,
That some suffer and some are in pain,
It isn't fair that some die so young,
Some are scarred, and yet some are so vain.

We can't do much to help these folk,
But there are others we can support.
By empathy, listening and prompting,
And by building up a rapport.

Someone who doesn't walk too well,
Can do a task with his fingers,
And as he shows someone else his skills,
He builds up a respect that lingers.

At fifty he is not 'over the hill'
But a fount of experience and knowing,
And if asked to pass just some of this on,
It results in two people growing.

Some have eyes that can no longer see,
But their ears work better than most
They hear the things that we may miss
The cry, the bravado, the boast.

We cannot end the suffering and pain
But we can all do our bit,
To make this world a fairer place
Where there's room for us all to fit.

Ann Tyas

CHILDREN ARE OUR FUTURE

All day long children are surrounded by violence,
On television, in papers, it makes no sense.
Violent behaviour in sport's glorified,
No wonder common decency has fled or died.

Children are our hope to create future harmony,
World of destructive behaviours all young see.
To have a chance, we must from violence abstain,
Or status quo, no matter how bad will remain.

S Mullinger

WORLD PEACE

I sought the wisdom-master,
By nations at war distressed.
He answered me as does a man
With heart and soul at rest;

And even as I listened,
I began to understand
That the words of truth he gave me
Were the same for every man.

'Men fight the outer dragon
Who have no peace within.
If you would heal the nations,
With yourself you must begin.

Strong are war's professionals
And theirs is the outer call,
But the influence of a man of peace
Is the strongest power of all.

He needs no trial or conquest
Who is by peace inspired.
Stand firm. You will win the battle
Without a shot fired.

Look to no outer factor
For the circumstance you rue:
What one does affects the all.
World peace begins with you.'

Pamela Constantine

HE'S HOME

His footsteps sound upon the path
My heart leaps to my throat
He's home again, he bangs the door
Drunkenly takes off his coat.

I try to fade into the wall
To avoid the pain I know will come
But to no avail, I feel his fist
Beating me like a drum.

It must end soon, is my last thought
As I slip down to the floor
The children dare not say a word
As they peep around the door.

What happened to the gentle man
I met as a shy young girl?
Who laughed and loved his way through life
And had my heart in a whirl.

All that's left is a wedding band
That lies like a weight on my hand
We have to get out, we have to be free
Or there's nothing left, for my children and me.

Pauline Nind

SEASONS OF LIFE

The seasons come and change your life around,
The autumn leaves turn from green to golden brown.
The wind catches them up, then throws them around,
Slowly falling to the ground,
Falling like my tears scattered around,
Tears bottled up for so many years
Like the seasons you come and go with my fears,
Like the leaves of autumn, and the cold winter snow,
You make my heart flutter as a butterfly's wings go.
But my heart has been broken
Like a young bird without flight,
My body feels crushed and without fight.
Like a dying rose you hold in your hand,
I see you before me, but I don't understand.
Oh my heart is in so much pain,
Please leave me in peace, alone again.
As my life is like the autumn leaves
Washed away by the rain
And I don't think I can start over again
Like the seasons of life are never the same.

Trudie Sullivan

THE MISSING MUSIC

What's happened to our songbirds?
The skylarks and the thrush
I remember days when a choir
Sang forth from every bush
A descant from every hedgerow
Or deep within the corn
Summer days were filled with music
From the slightest crack of dawn
The sun would push its head up
To the blackbirds' early call
To strike up the morning chorus
To sing out for one and all
Now the morns are growing silent
Not many left to croon
Between the early morning sunrise
And the showing of the moon

Brian Wardle

WHY?

As they strolled through the park
One sunny day,
The child turned to her mother
And this did say:
'Why does the grass
Grow green and tall?
Why do the leaves
In autumn fall?
Where do butterflies
Go at night?
Who tells the sun
To shine so bright?
Who taught the blackbird
How to fly?
Who tells the flowers
When they must die?'

The mother smiled
As she answered her child,
'It's Mother Nature
Who takes care of the wild.'

A J Hunter

TIME KNOCKS IMPATIENT

Earth's resources,
Sustain life's forces,
Continually abuse them,
We will lose them.

Time knocks impatient,
At the future's door,
With an urgency,
We cannot ignore.

Devina Symes

What Manner Of Love?

I know it is of a truth
We name them
Natural disasters, forces of nature
But He removes the mountains
And they know not
Which overturns them in his anger
Which shakes the earth
Out of her place
And the pillars thereof
And commands the sun
And it rises
And seals up the stars
Which alone spreads out the heavens
And treads upon the waves of the sea
My finite mind cannot reason out
His infinite wisdom
For he is not a man
As I am
You have granted me life and favour
Clothes me with skin and flesh
And hast fenced me with bones and sinews
If I be wicked woe unto me
And if I be righteous
Yet will I lift up my head.

Ebenezer Essuman

MINDLESS

Rubbish, rubbish all around
Chewed up gum stuck to the ground,
People not thinking where rubbish is tossed
This selfish attitude makes me cross.
Wildlife getting injured, some even die
It makes me angry, it makes me cry.
Rivers and streams with rubbish dumped in
People don't care to use the bin.
What will we do when plagued with rats
Hope they'll be caught by our pet cats?
Stop and think is all I ask
Before this rubbish becomes our ugly mask.

Angie

PLACEBO

Today is a hurry of robotic machinations
Earthbound fortunes made on tortured gains
Manic mouths threatening steel and
Throwing out orgies of telelvisions and things.
We are always flickering on and off switches
Cabling together days of yore, built on ore
The devil it has become grins at us from where we placed it
Heavy stretched nylon silence we raped the earth with
Drowning the mountain of unmoveables, spewing back
The wretched thing we gave it.

The grin it has become has power:
Once it amazed us, like a steam train
Ferreting holes in hills:
Now it is placebo for all our ills
Demon-caused and stirring the millennium back to earth.
We can never escape the magic eye that talks
Or erase the bliss of the sky we walk in:
The big connection here draws us into star birth
Where we live, wet and wild, like a caveman's dream.

Julie Ashpool

THE EARTH WE LIVE ON

Litter should not be thrown
on the Earth we adore
for it creates mess
which I abhor.

Recycled household waste
and the use of a bike,
instead of a car
is what the Earth would like.

To save our environment
there's plenty we can do.
With time and effort spent
from people like me and you.

The way we treat our environment
is a habit we can break,
providing we work together,
is all that it would take.

Our planet is so precious
so we all must strive
to protect it for the future
and keep it alive.

If everybody made a change,
there'd be so much space
on this beautiful Earth
which we should no longer waste.

Shabnam Yasmin (Baz)

OUR WORLD IN FOCUS

What passion and such conflicting scientific information
Global warming, climate changes severe problems for every nation

International conferences, protestors' violent demonstrations
Remind us of the doubts and fears of possible world devastations

Magnificent tropical rainforests completely ruined by deforestation
Changes in ocean levels encroaching on landmasses damaging
habitations

Mother Nature plays her part in our planet Earth's decimation
Flooding, droughts, earthquakes, hurricanes and such like devastation

Urgent action must be taken to save our world's possible destruction
First priority reduce emissions and pollutions by industrial and
commercial institutions

Change the way of living in this consumer throw away society
Join the revolution, protect your beautiful planet leaving it fit
for the future generation

K G Johnson

I TALK TO THE TREES . . .

We voted for the Tories,
They seemed so squeaky-clean!
We voted for more teachers,
But we never voted Green.

We listened to the Bishop,
We answered to the Dean,
We shouted Hallelujah,
But we never prayed for Green.

Some voted for the Euro,
We voted for the Queen,
We voted for the Liberals,
But we never voted Green.

We asked for extra pensions,
We hadn't got a bean,
We asked for cheaper petrol,
But we never asked for Green.

We voted for the NHS
And trains to Aberdeen,
We went and voted Labour,
But we never voted Green.

They thanked us for our trouble,
Then the Government Machine
Took away our children's future
With a law that banished Green.

Peter Davies

Rich And Poor

What shall we hand over to our children?
What will future generations think of us,
We will leave a world divided and torn,
With underlying strife between rich and poor,
A continuing battle of the haves and the have nots,
Counties so rich and careless who pollute at will,
Others so poor, it's a struggle to plant the crops and pay the bill,
Many of these poorer countries are ruled by tyrants or despots.

We will leave a hole in the ozone layer,
Which grows bigger each day,
Climatic changes which are beyond our comprehension,
Species of animals and plants slip from the eco chain,
We leave wild beasts with less and less space, they survive in vain,
Still we pollute in our own backyard,
We import and export atomic waste as if it were confetti,
Hauling it from one end of the land to the other,
On a specially built underailable train.

We are born to this world,
Spend our four score years and ten,
Then depart to who knows where or when,
I wish we could honestly say,
When we leave it's a far better place,
But sadly in so many areas that is not the case,
In the great scheme of things,
Mother Nature cuts our cloth and lets us out to play.

Money is everything, money is god,
We all fall under its spell,
Following in one form or another its golden trail,
But no amount of money could buy
A fresh clear dawn breaking on the bay,
Or a million spiders' webs precisely placed on a cold
                                    and frosty morning
No amount of money could be collected,
To reproduce a sunset, or fill a dusty plane with vegetation,
Or replace the rainforest no matter how hard we try.

P J Littlefield

THE WORLD IS OURS

The world is ours,
To guard and love,
To do our part
In our own way,
Treat our land, with
Great respect, like a
Flower garden in spring.
Our time on Earth,
May be quite short,
But we will know,
We did our best to show,
We loved this land
And never will we allow,
If we are there,
Litter to appear, in
Town, country, or by the sea.
We promise our children,
We will teach, to follow
In our way.
Our voices to be joined by theirs,
Will make it swell
Into a loud roar.
So for the generations
To come, this earth
In focus will be.

Audrey Allen

SEA MYSTERIES

Just listening to the sea roaring in,
And pounding on the pebbled beach.
Throwing up driftwood and seaweed,
Then dragging the stones in retreat!

For somehow its power and strength,
Seems to be calming on the mind.
Here's something man had no power over,
Its domination and mysteries undefined!

It is hard to believe there's life beneath,
As most of us only see it from above.
But beneath the wave a world so beautiful,
So different, magical and full of love!

No busy traffic or cluttered streets,
Just sand, coral and rocks to explore.
Seaweed waving in the passing currents,
Plus all the sea creatures we adore!

But afraid we are only land creatures
So can only invade this world for a while,
It is lucky they can't see our way of life,
The dirt and pollution wouldn't make them smile!

Ann Beard

NEW DAWN

If I leave behind the animal meat
and nurture myself on fruit, grain and wheat.
If I can stop the pain of one beast near death
then the dawn will break with a softer breath.

If I keep just one creature from the terror of the kill
and live from the produce of earth's bountiful fill.
If I can keep the panic from just one creature's heart
then the dawn will break with a gentler start.

If we could hear the desperate cries through the slaughterhouse wall
and watch the terrified creature take its last fatal fall.
If we could choose not to do this to the helpless in their plight
then the dawn would break with a brighter light.

Patricia Calder

THE COST OF POLLUTION FOR THE FUTURE

In the future will family meals be a thing of the past
Sitting together at table, how long will it last?
As more and more people snack out or eat alone in the day
Microwaved food has resulted in quick eating from a tray.

Sometimes I envisage a cupboard containing a few jars
With different cellulose-based swelling tablets shaped like stars
Each point dissolving vitamins, minerals, some proteins too.
Land and sea so polluted what else could the scientists do?

Mary Beale

SALVATION

In the beginning I was with my Father
and as I travelled the path of my soul
I met Evolution.
From the seeds of time grew Population
and by his side stood Saturation.
Over the land of Ignorance walked the
giant Starvation.

Lost in the forest of Confusion I fought
hand to hand with Pollution, but my heart
lay heavy in the shadow of Humiliation.
In Desolation I dreamed of Revolution.

Out of the darkness came Recreation and
I embraced the Solution. My body lived with
Compassion and from my mouth spoke
Communication.
Through the eyes of my Mother shone
Inspiration and all around on the earth,
under the sea and in the heavens was the
everlasting Conclusion, Salvation.

Brendan G Ryan

AN UNHEARD PRAYER

At least once a day,
My thoughts stray,
To the unfortunate world outside,
Where intelligence seems to portray,
A lack of moral sway,
There's not enough care,
For those born in squalor or fear,
Too many for the world to cope,
Lost of Love, Attention and Hope,
How I wish the whole world would respond,
And destroy all weapons and arms,
To allow each a life without harm,
That's the strength of my prayer from beyond.

It seems not to be heard,
How can one spread the word?
Impossible, I fear,
Because nobody wants to hear,
Life does not matter,
In this world of patter,
Only monetary gains portray,
The worth of life today.

Barbara R Lockwood

In The Lapland Mountains

There is movement coming over the seeping cairns
Tumbling upon the horizon sun,
Mountains reign here, outlaying the Lapland flow,
Rushing to sustain these magnetic attitudes.

But here, there is reflecting brilliance pure air
The world lusting to snap up the violate space
Like a strange, crinkled, garnished wilderness,
Leering around the Lapland's mountains.

Beautiful scenes of silver haze,
Shining about on promised land
Watching the hidden mountains
Peering through the surface.

Giving together those majestic Lapland mountains
With glory sunbeam shine
Midsummer is a long, long day
In this fragmented sight.

Heather Aspinall

DESECRATORS

Clover, like the four leaf flutter of my heart
Orchids hiding not from bees but bullies
And dandelion, a puff-ball of parachutes that fall to earth
To mingle with muddy boots and the cowpats of society.
Bludgeon me with burdock, or poison me with nightshade
Deadly or otherwise.
I will survive as surely as grass grows
Or groundweed that covers the covert land.
The earth does not belong to us
We belong to the earth.
I will still dance with the harebell fairy
And lay alone in the bluebell wood
Walk on the bare, atomic sands
And search the sea for puffins or pollution.
Despots undermine my courage
But as I wigwam my way, you will not break my resolve
Like grey owl or running bear - ungodly heroes
I will stand to attention when the wind howls
Or the river bursts its banks.
At the chosen time my spirit will ride roughshod
Through the stars
And my soul will return to haunt you -

Jennifer H Fox

BLUE WORLD

Two thousand years have passed, alas
We view the spectrum through rose-tinted glass
Man has progressed in leaps and bounds
Turning our precious world upside down
Flying through the heavens to descend upon the moon
Realising our blue planet, a gifted, golden spoon
But knowing that man could be its final ruin
Love, truth and peace, our everlasting tune
People so precious, as they journey on and on
Through the darkness, a golden light will surely be shone
Guiding mankind to where they belong
Peace and love be our kingdom of song
Changes come, yes man has to grow
Like the gardener of life, a seed he must sow
Kindness, strength and love, row upon row
New life springs up, mankind has to bow
Life so precious every last strand
Hold on to the values that enrich the promised land
Heart upon heart, hand to hand
Remembering as our Saviour lay dying
It was his last stand and command.

Katherine Quaye

JUST A TIP

Sunlight, shimmering on the lake,
Where people sit and take a break,
Peace and quiet, not a sound,
What a wonderful haven we have found.

Wind rippling gentle little waves,
That trickle along the shore like slaves,
Bringing rubbish like dog brings stick,
It's enough to make one sick.

Plastic bags, tin cans too,
All left here to spoil the view,
By selfish people who came to see,
This wonderful place as so did we.

So now it looks like just a tip,
And wasn't even worth the trip.

G W Bailey

TIMES PAST

You ask me how a hundred years have seemed
To those of us who lived them - truth to tell
We took them in our stride as mortals do
I don't remember much of them too well.

We had as many wars, I think, as ever.
We had respect for those who brought us through.
There's not much difference in people either;
Forever looking for new things to do.

And so we had our pressure groups to prick
Authorities and older verities.
We went for acupuncture, therapies
To needle folk into activity.

But now we've found a different game to play
There are no rules as far as I can see.
You get your thrills sitting before a screen
By tapping at the laptop on your knee.

Reality is not the sense we thought,
Of touch and feeling, light in people's eyes;
It is now virtual on the internet
You really do not need to move to live.

Cut us not off from our humanity
Time is continuous, not governed by
The passing of our months and hours and days,
Equating grammar to eternity.

Does 'Carmen' still play at the Albert Hall?
Is love more than unbalanced chemicals?
Is Armageddon close, or can we call
Man's bluff? He gets it wrong as usual.

Joan Gordon

THINK ABOUT IT

Why is there so much conflict in the world?
That man cannot enjoy the miraculous things
Cannot your neighbour step foot over his boundary?
Can he not come and admire your part of the planet
Without wanting to seize it?

Do you not invite him over for a chat and a feast
To talk about the wonders of the world?
Have we come this far, and learned nothing about mankind
How to help each other and live together?

Is there not a piece of blue sky
For each and everyone to look up to?
Or enough space for everyone to walk in his own country
Without wanting to snatch a piece of his neighbours?

What grow you in yours?
Do you have something to spare, and share
With people living in a neighbouring country
Which is barren?
Could you help irrigate their land, of which they know nothing
But are willing to learn?

What right does one man have, to take the life of another?
Just because the victim didn't share his views
Or wouldn't hand over his hard-earned cash.
And why is it, too many children suffer so much abuse?
Be it violent or emotional
They didn't ask to come here
We should cherish them, nurture them, guide them
In this confusing world
What legacy do we leave them? Think about it.

Edith Crumb

TODAY

Today I saw a peacock strutting positively,
shiny blue neck stuck out,
cross the road in front of us carefully,
fully aware that we were there.

We drove on towards the Indian burial grounds
through the valley of the trees,
each tree more precious in this desert country
than any nuclear bomb revered and unaware
nestling in its nearby hideout.

I remembered a trumpet once, abandoned in a field,
needing a trumpeter to rival the calling of that peacock
or raise the grass around those Indian mounds
or sound out the dreadful trump of doom
if any trumpeter could be found to play that tune.

Pam Redmond

TAKE TIME

It amazes me, every day of my life
To see so much bustle, so much strife
It all seems speeded up somehow
No time for thought, it's now, now, now.

Everyone is travelling, rushing somewhere
Doesn't anyone take time to stop and stare
At a beautiful sunset, a laughing child
Kittens playing, a landscape so wild.

No one ever has time to simply talk
To use their legs, not the car, and walk
Can't anyone sit and watch the sea
Stop racing around, stay still, just be.

Too much noise, too little peace
How can we give this world release
From war and hate and dreadful waste
All brought about by too much haste.

If we sat in silence and let in thought
We'd see the harm stupid man has wrought
This planet, our home, is falling apart
What we need to do is heal her heart.

Is there an answer somewhere out there
To a sad and lonely human prayer?
That some day soon every man will see
The tragic waste upsetting me.

Will anyone ever stand up and say
This is all our fault, now we must pay?
We must stop the rot, begin again
And try to make our Earth, our friend.

Carolyn Fittall

SAVE OUR ENVIRONMENT

Picture this
Morning mist
Echoing cuckoos
Crying in the distance
Sparrows singing in tune
Crow Wood personal to me
Wild flowers disappearing like skylarks
Listen to Mother Nature.

Alan Hattersley

SETTING THE RECORD STRAIGHT

'Hello Mrs Jones, how yer doing', are you well,
where is Thomas today?'
These are the nice, friendly greetings, exchanged as I wind on my way.

Over yonder I may see Aunt Edith as I pedal on over the hill
Making her way to the butcher's, for some rump for my old Uncle Bill.

It's nice when I'm turning those pedals,
round the lanes to the shops or the pub
Or off road through the mud and the shingle,
then on home for a bath and a scrub.

Whether turning those wheels nice and gentle
or pumping the heart at a pace
I enjoy from the seat of my cycle,
real fresh air and a great sense of space.

You don't have to feel too embarrassed, you also can get on yer bike
For short journeys you will find it quicker,
I'm sure once you try it you'll like it.

But get one thing straight from the outset; I am not about banishing cars
I have found that despite all the traffic I can travel about like a star.

Some may say that the bike is for poor folk,
but I am richer in spirit and mind
I have found independence and freedom
and at times leave those motors behind.

Martin Farbrother
'The Bard of Sturry'

WINNER TAKES ALL . . .

The millennium's now upon us
the Age of Aquarius dawns.
The Piscean Age is dying
with a past that few will mourn.

We dream of final battles
where Good triumphs over sin.
We dream of Second Comings.
We dream that God will win . . .

We gaze at our pregnant future
like a mother, praising birth;
but maybe a smirking changeling lurks
with its fey, unhuman mirth.

So we should look more closely -
Reality's not well.
As things now stand, the truth is -
this planet's bound for hell.

We take more than entitlement;
encourage entropy.
We over-harvest oceans.
We shape our destiny.

If human greed continues,
and careless, we pursue
the ends that we're hell-bent on,
God knows what God may do . . .

So Eternity's at stake here;
but too finite are man's schemes.
I see Aquarian hope being stalked
by the devil's wildest dreams . . .

Jenny Proom

DUMPED

Unceremoniously dumped, rubbish is everywhere,
thoughtlessly scattered, without a single care.
Eternal plastic, rubber made to last,
empty tin cans and broken glass.

Kicking material, for kids on the streets,
scalpels, for children's unprotected feet.
Death-traps for fishes in the blue seas,
a pain in the arse, for gardeners like me.

Strewn across countryside, lush and green,
dumpers of rubbish, are so terribly mean.
Depriving new generations, of earth's beauty,
dumping them, into the hands of the law,
would be a privilege, not to mention a duty.

Andy Monnacle

PULLING TOGETHER

As we look around us
Wherever we may dwell,
There is much that should concern us
With sights that stories tell.

Rubbish in the hedgerows
Litter in the streets.
Wanton damage in the parks
Such things we all do meet.

Such things seem very minor
When on a larger scale,
So many larger issues
The environment oft doth fail.

Rules to follow seem in vain
For no one seems to care,
Responsibility is shelved
The blame we all must share.

Example can be shown by all
This is how the children learn,
To solve their many problems
It is to us they turn.

So let us pull together
Our part however small,
Will help to make this world of ours
A safer place for all.

F L Brain

EARTH SEASONS

So cool the wind that excludes feeling.
Drives mere sentiment from the soul.
Makes your world a hollow numbness,
Become an android? An unfeeling goal.

Sun and fire, what a comfort.
Seduced by their warmth and power.
Fall under a spell of utter luxury.
Climb into your ivory tower.

But dreary grey clouds. Misery.
Not again. Its started to rain.
Morale plummets at the mere mention.
Get the washing in again.

Planet greens and seasons change,
Can I convert you, any hope?
A living earth is all around you.
Better than watching your TV soap.

Do you get my drift of meaning,
Break away from the plastic herd.
Understand this world of beauty.
Consumer society is so absurd!

Sing you birds. Hello, good morning.
It's welcome to another day.
Fill your thoughts with smiling sweetness.
Let your mind roll in the hay.

Forget the paper and the TV.
Become one with Mother Earth.
Unite with the strength of nature.
Come alive, it's time for rebirth.

B Haswell

THINGS WE TAKE FOR GRANTED

A fiery sky as the sun is about to set;
silver moons reflection on a calm, dark sea,
The colourful rainbow the sun makes to chase the rain away,
Children's laughter, dancing feet,
smiles from strangers you pass on the street,
The smell of the countryside, fresh, clean air,
the feel of the breeze combing through your hair,
The dark, velvet sky, with stars twinkling bright,
lover's caresses on just such a night,
A baby's touch, soft, gentle and warm,
kisses and hugs tiny arms round your neck,
Families, strong together as they brave out a storm,
each link in a chain that never gets worn,
A roof over your head, freedom of speech,
food in your belly, clothes on your back, shoes on your feet,
Legs to walk on, eyes to see, ears to hear with,
arms to hold, lips to speak, truth be told,
In this world where everyone runs,
much too busy to stop . . . and have fun,
Take a second or two to look and see,
all the spectacular things that's there for free,
Landscapes and rivers, flowers and trees,
babies bouncing on Grandma's knees,
It's all there for you each day of the year,
open your eyes and stare in awe,
Don't take these things for granted anymore . . . please!

Helen Posgate

In A World Of Peace

In a world of peace,
There would be no war.
No time for fighting,
No death anymore.

In a world of peace,
There would always be light.
Shining throughout,
The day and night.

In a world of peace,
There would be no hunger.
No one starving,
No famine for the younger.

In a world of peace,
There would always be smiles.
Lots of happy faces,
That go on for miles.

In a world of peace,
There would be no hate.
Between all the religions,
From now until fate.

In a world of peace,
There would always be love.
In this new-found world,
Watching from above.

Jamie Barnes

WHERE HAVE THEY GONE?

Where are the people, cycling for pleasure?
Domed-hatted bobbies, riding at leisure.
Convoys of trucks race along, without care.
The stench of fumes trails into the air!

Where are the owners of the allotment bed?
Are they all eating junk food, instead?
Obese blobs with eyes glued to a square.
Burgers and pizzas and unhealthy fare!

Where are all the lush fields of years ago?
Buttercups and cowslips no longer grow!
Brick boxes that have no garden around.
Greedy profiteers use up all the ground!

Where are the streets that once looked so dapper?
Bottles and cans and discarded wrapper!
Unwanted lunches rot in the gutter.
Who will abolish all this clutter?

Where are the houses, built on chemical spill?
Their owners, inside them sickly and ill!
Who will start to care about human life?
Who will hear the earth crying out in strife?

Where are the ones recycling household waste?
And home-grown vegetables long to taste!
Making healthy compost to feed their plants
To give the produce to uncles and aunts!

Where are the wise ones who hold pollution at bay?
To save our planet for a future day!
So, all sit up, take notice and be stirred!
Before there are no voices to be heard!

Val Spall

CAN NATURE NURTURE

Divorced from nature,
With wrongful knowledge of supremacy.
Forgetting the theory of Darwin.
We are nature and nature will attack.

Chernobyl's fall-out.
For animals to graze,
To fertilise all plant life and unsanitised streams.
Vegetarian or omnivore, each one of us trapped.

Senses concealed
While we desperately earn, in unnatural light.
Ending up needing some Freudian psyche.
No other species need analysed dreams.

Waters are rising
And climates affected by deforestation.
The third world suffers through power and greed,
Where profits allow uncompromised wealth.

Divorced from nature.
Is our fate predestined or supremacy strong.
Will our remnants become as fossilised fuel,
Encapsulated and stored by a museum of earth.

Maria Bernadette Potter

BLOT ON THE LANDSCAPE

Paths hugging the river banks, and weaving between the trees,
blackberry pickers, give way to worker bees.
Anglers casting lines in quiet anticipation,
fishes study fishing hooks with due consideration.

Ramblers strolling along designated tracks.
Majestic swans and families of ducks,
vie with each other for tasty little snacks.
Shy little creatures keeping out of reach.

Graceful bushy-tailed squirrels dart from tree to tree,
timid little field mice playing hide and seek.
Cyclist overtaking walkers pass the time of day,
dogs and their owners coming out to play.

The density of the foliage filters out the sun,
all the little children having lots of fun.
It's surely perfection for the majority of users,
spoilt only by litter discarded by the minority of abusers.

Brenda Rollo

WARMING UP

Sodden fields cling
like wet velvet.
Rock below the melting clay
shines and seeps catarrh.
Earth gasps tepid days
as drizzle sieves from overloaded clouds.

Things are stirring in the soil.
Cattle, innocent deceived cannibals
add their ordure to the mulch
and black spores germinate, mutate
as poisoned mites we cannot see.

So fences sprout and gates are closed.
Footpaths rest unwalked.
Where sheep were dipped, formaldehyde
anoints tyres wiped with straw
and only rain and crowcall
break the sorrow of the fields.

'No need to worry' chants Dives from the setting sun
stoking his furnaces, gulping fossil fuels,
dazzling the surface with the real fools' gold.
The villages and moorlands hear his call
while farmers dig their trenches deep,

feel hunger bite, tear down towers and weep.
In the same sad key the ghosts of Eynam wail,
pits split apart, give up their dead.
Bells clang, slow carts appear,
red crosses blaze on doors again.

John H Hope

CANDLELIGHT

Candles, not an invention of today, but of ages past,
but what is it in their glowing ray, that in this frenetic
world, by their soothing light we, in our daily fight
are cast into a stillness of the now?

Longingly, lovingly, we embrace their glow,
releasing tensions that flow from hearts devoid
of rest and peace, and in their gentle ray fears
decrease their hold on yesterday.

Brightly burning flickering flame, you hold our
gaze, and our hearts, once more aflame with
life, are grateful for your dancing ray
partnering strife with new hope for tomorrow.

Blessed light, soothing, calming, dancing before us
in our lives with promise bright; so small your flame,
yet your glowing constancy, guiding us aright,
so to strain our eyes on eternity.

Catherine Riley

UNBLEST

Stand full arrayed
amidst the wavering shower;
turn here and there to spy your mark
that of the earth in its dreaming dark.
So unfamiliar, so without amaze
her wondering languorous gaze.
The chilly truth of stars I can forgo
and, back from that void I shrink in fear,
this kind of world is all I know.
All beauteous things for which I love
by laws of space and time decay,
but oh, the very reason why
I clasp them is because they die.
To one another, for all the world
we here as on a darkling plain
no certitude, peace, nor help from pain
Ignorant armies clash by night
distracted and like us unblest,
city by city - the square - the houses! Why?
And the stars a'saunter by.

Peter Higgs

WINGS OF DAWN

Lying in the stillness of anticipation
I savour the drink of trepidation
I await the wings of dawn.
The dark curtain rises revealing
chill, fresh new light.
Gone the night.

Suddenly from nowhere it seems
The solitary call, real not dreams.
I hear the wings of dawn.
The first bird sweet calling
shrill, bright new song.
come on, come on.

Crystal-clear birdsong, clear blue sky
another bird answers from somewhere nigh.
I hear the chorus of dawn.
the orchestration of birdsong
responding, uniting,
We come, we come.

Walking in the stillness of anticipation
I savour the drink of trepidation
I approach the wings of dawn.
The grey bird lies resting,
chill, dormant and quiet
Awaiting the flight.

Suddenly from no certain places.
People and passports and cases.
The awakening of dawn,
The first stewardess calling
The first engine roaring, come on come on.

Mary Farrant

GREAT BRITAIN

A small island
Of empty fields
And barren hearts.
 Do the angels weep?

We had dominion
Over the animals,
They were in our care.
 Do the angels weep?

We exploited them
Huge herds and flocks
Closed abattoirs.
 Do the angels weep?

'We must make more profit
From pigs and cows and sheep'
Does it matter
 If the angels weep?

G Poole

THE WORLD AS I SEE IT

The world no longer consists of nature and beauty
The constant abuse of our surroundings has left it plain and empty

There no longer is an undiscovered place that lays untouched from
the hand of destruction for everything has been poisoned
to consist of hate and anger

Innocence no longer lays in a child's mind for we have all been
exposed to the world of lies.

Sara Clendinning

MY WISH

My search lies
within the petals,
uncurl gently each one to see
the priceless jewels held herein-
and the mysterious, exquisite beauty

Through infinite heavens
my wish soars
and beats dream rhythms
under Pegasus' wing
- filling the hearts
of each living thing

My wish is colours
 - in rainbow hue
Peace for the world,
and a wish for you!

My wish is contained in
a unicorn birth
To bring spring forever,
and joy to the Earth . . .

Tracie Ellis

MY CAMERA'S FOCUSED

As I focus the lens of my camera what do I see?
A world with no pity, turned by a rusty key.
The forlorn, the sick at the bottom of the pile
No one prepared to go that extra mile.

Where is the mercy we long to behold
Will no one speak, will no one be bold?
I turn the focus, I focus for hope
But all I see is drugs and dope.

What was the cause of all this dismay?
How did it happen along this way?
Were not guidelines laid down in the past
They don't have to be all that vast.

Necessary, neat, tidy, complete
That would be an amazing feat.
Now my lens comes into focus again
Ah! no more sickness, no more pain.

And as I press the shutter down
I see a king that wears a crown.
His rule is caring, his rule is just
My lens in focus is now a must.

Denise Shaw

JUST THINKING

My young grandson, Josh, he's not quite three,
What kind of world will he live to see.
Thinking back to my own childhood days,
Things have changed a lot, in many ways.
Fish and chips were wrapped in newspaper,
Bread could only be bought from the baker.
Milk came in glass bottles, right to your door,
You left a note if you wanted one more.
There was no junk mail to fill up the bin,
No banana diet to make you thin.
No aerosol sprays to hide the smell,
No NHS when you slipped and fell.
No microwave for a quick bite to eat,
No loud music with a thumping beat.
Now, of course, nearly everyone owns
Compact disc players, and mobile phones,
And it's plastic this, and plastic that;
Nobody has the time for a chat.
They're too busy driving from A to B,
Telling everyone that they want to be free.
Some say the world is a better place,
For the changes made by the human race;
While others will tell you the end is nigh
And, the world as we know it, soon will die.
The changes now are coming much faster;
Will man, or nature, be the master?

Geraldine Parr

EARTH TO EARTH

Twisting and snaking in soil, new life waking;
Tiny shoots twining and breaking into being.
Reaching and stretching, strengthened by the sun
That shines on every one of us, seeing
The flowers bursting into bloom, assume the colours
Of the rainbows that arch across the sky.
Porcelain petals dripping dew, bees sipping pollen;
Buzzing their languorous lullaby.
Blades of grass cutting swathes beneath the trees,
Boughs swaying while the winds blow;
Coursing through the leaves like water over reeds,
Branches shading rippled glades below.
Treetops shyly rustling to the birds bustling
Within their emerald hair, waving hazily;
From the nests appearing warblers on the wing,
Beaks and feathers veering crazily.
Higher yet they swoop and climb into the sunshine,
Silhouetted spirits projected onto blue;
Soaring where only scoops of cloud have ever flown,
That drift and glide, hiding things from view.
Floating silently in pale seas of violet,
Whirling into storms of ice beyond mountain heights;
Here the atmosphere bites rushing into space,
Led by ruby fire and sapphire lights.
Exploding like blossom garlands above the earth,
Rained upon by shooting stars and meteor showers;
The world a shiny marble rolled into the soil,
Lying beneath the sunshine and the flowers.

Jonathan Goodwin

CHANGING TIMES

I take my mind back to yesteryears
Some thirty odd years ago
The cane field was our livelihood
So I had to do my share
Those days were gleeful
For we chatted as we worked
Our tastebuds were satisfied
For the cane juices were our mates.
Today living has no match
On what life used to be
For technology have taken away our work
Now gladness has gone away
Our world today needs a helping hand
To restore the damage that's been done
For the air is polluted
And men are dying quicker than they should
My yesteryears were happier than those of today
For fun galore had walked with me
Now a computer has befriended me
And my words are typed each day
But I'll rather be in that cane field any day

Carolie Pemberton

NOWHERE TO GO

Nowhere to go, nowhere to hide
No cosy nest, my wife beside
Scant are the hedgerows, scant and thin
No safe place to nest within
Men their big sharp cutters wield
Chop off branches that would shield
Wearily flying to find a place,
To carry on the feathered race.

Nowhere to go, nowhere to run
Nobody cares about poor old Bun
Fields with even longer furrow
Nowhere for poor old me to burrow
We really do not do much harm
We're part and parcel of the farm
You get your fun when us you shoot
So please do not put in the boot.

Nowhere to go, nowhere to fly
So we can spy, with beady eye
A tasty vole in course rough grass
Without them barn owls cannot last
Farmers plough right to the edge
Please leave us a little wedge
Where voles can multiply and thrive
So owls like me can stay alive.

Nowhere to go, no woodland glade
Cool and dark with dappled shade
Woodland animals and flowers
Do we see our final hours?
When men with unrelenting sway
Takes our habitat away
Can't we all live side by side
In an idyllic countryside?

Dora Watkins

GUILT TRIP

Just take a look around
What do you see?
Old burnt-out cars
Rubbish on the side.
A seed trying hard
To grow through the earth,
Needs all it's strength
From the rubbish we throw.
Do we see
Are we blind
Why? do people leave their garbage behind.
For every tree that is cut
Every cry is heard,
Leave our land to grow naturally.
Why is it we see
At the seaside our tea
Chip paper not put in the bin.
Our land is our home
Therefore we must keep
The carpets of nature
To grow and to live.
Culprits we are
We have all done the crime,
It's for us to teach
And not to become blind.
So let us go out
And see what's to be done
Make this world a cleaner, greener place
For everyone.

Alison Hitch

MAN THE CURSE

The Sun
glowing and grinning
sighting and lighting
Yet, who taught it to burn?
Burn and blister its own fleshes.

The Sea
dashing and splashing
drifting and greeting
Yet, who taught it to slaughter?
Slaughter and slay its very soul.

The Forest
growing and gleaming
variegating and shifting
Yet, who taught it to erode?
Erode and sever its own heart.

Who?
makes

> the sun *burn*
> the sea *slaughter*
> the forest *erode*

Who is the fool?
Fool enough to destroy
his very treasures

Man

Jiwamalar Perumal

DOESN'T ANYONE CARE?

Crisp bags,
Sweet wrappers,
Does no one care
Anymore?
Just throw them down
On the floor.

Spray cans,
Graffiti,
Does no one care
For the wall?
Just leave the bricks,
Let it fall.

Seashores,
Woodland walks,
Does no one care
If they last?
Just carry on,
Spurn the past.

Trees gone,
Bird songs cease,
Does no one care
No one mind?
Just carry on.
Are they blind?

Still time,
Turn things around,
Show that you care,
Let's all say
Don't carry on
Same old way!

Angela Pritchard

GLOBAL WARMING

Smoky factory chimneys, pushing fumes into the sky,
The ozone layer thinning it's enough to make one cry,
Nuclear reactor stations are poisoning the soil,
Great big heavy tankers making slicks of oil,
Chemicals and hormones washed into the streams,
Oh it's not real, it can't be true, I see it in my dreams,
Just don't forget the skin care, whenever you go out,
Must keep yourself protected each time the sun's about,
It's acid rain that's falling to soften up the earth,
And hail the size of golf balls bound down for all they're worth,
And they're no longer small and clear, the way they used to be,
They thunder down out of the sky, and knock you off your feet,
There's flooding and famine in lands far away,
Here gas-guzzling cars, are the thing of the day,
While ice caps are melting the rivers overflow,
The fields are all flooding, cos it's nowhere to go,
Caused by global warming, the weather people say,
We will all suffer later, when some price we will pay.

B Smith

CRIMAC

Trapped en-route, it's baking, not cool.
Steaming horns and honking fume.
Rainbow colours in dreadful array.
Juggernaut's tread leaves nobody room.
This midday convoy of drama and gloom.
Life can be cruel - motors rule!

I call it 'crimac', this hasty intent.
A wish to run free brings an outcome of stress.
I am a party, but so is my need.
Travelling forward, it's onward we press.
Driving you guess, in coachwork we dress.
The tickets we've spent, people are bent.

Crimac is splashed where trees graced the air,
On through each parish in shires of the land.
Sacrificial fauna succumbs to machine.
One-way destruction this power at hand,
Like bombs from the nimbus to pummel the sand.
Why can't we share, with crimac to spare?

S Pete Robson

A Place Of Dreams

A path runs down to the sandy shore
With towering cliffs above and around
Encircled by the turquoise-blue water of a Cornish sea.
Little white waves endlessly lapping the beach
Shells like bright jewels cling to the rocks
Little pools, miniature gardens with darting fish
Anemones of rainbow shades and deadly tentacles
Great strands of tough brown seaweed
Glossy with sea spray and the tang of the sea
Overhead are the shrill cries of gulls on the wing
As they swoop far into the ocean
At the top of the cliff is a field of flowers in profusion
A Persian carpet of pink thrift, blue of harebell and scabious
With trailing vetches of yellow and purple
And the sweet fragrance of thyme
Butterflies hover to sup the sweet nectar
Only the murmur of bees, the swell of the waves
And the warmth of the sun
From a dazzling blue sky flecked with clouds
Let me drift into sleep
This is indeed a place of dreams
But a lovely dream come true.

Elisabeth Morley

THE MAGIC BEAN (THE MUCANA BEAN)

Have you seen the magic bean?
You may, perhaps, know what I mean.
No - not the pantomime
that you see at Christmastime.
Someone cleverer than our Jack!
who climbed the beanstalk.
although he had also quite the knack
of himself making quite a show,
without ever using a hoe!

But - now - in Guatemala and Brazil,
hungry children can now eat their fill,
because of someone's great discovery
for our good Earth's recovery.

A magic bean has been found,
which when planted in the ground
will now help other plants to grow -
The mucana bean - sown in a row!
A little foil,
to help the soil
not to erode
from its own abode;
putting back the minerals we all need;
too, just from this tiny little seed for you.

So - here are my words of praise
to those whose work will help erase
the threat to all of us on this planet -
We needed a miracle - and some have done it!

Bea Wilson

THE BRAVE

It's so easy to forget what has been done.
Just remembered once a year, all those who have gone.
But to all those that suffered trouble and strife
God bless you, I thank you, I owe you my life!
Each and every year through
I always thank you
'The brave'.

Your devotion to your country and your kin, I admire
The motto 'never give in; set all men's; hearts afire!
We cherish and respect you forever, so clear,
For without you, our 'brave men' I would not be here!
I'll always think of you
and all that you've been through
'The brave'.

As a war baby orphan I reflect on my life
And give thanks to the heroes who gave all for me and my wife
I can't thank you enough for what you have done
'May the Lord be with you' my Queen's Servicemen, you are No 1!
What helped me survive
and kept me alive
were 'The Brave'.

As long as I live I will never ever forget
'The freedom' that you gave me, never taken for granted, But yet?
I will always give thanks and respect for all that you gave
As long as I live, my saviours, our country, you saved!
The lives that you gave -
The memories we save!
For 'The brave' - Never forgotten! Amen.

Tony W Rylatt

HELP!

Here in the west, the life that we embrace
is filled with opportunities galore.
While every road leads to our resting place
our duty en-route is contributor
towards the dream the world is striving for.

We need to end hostilities of nations,
make poverty a problem of the past,
endeavour to enjoy good race relations,
join in a pact of peace that's sworn to last
and learn to understand culture-contrast.

We should all care for our environment,
return to animals, their right to graze,
abolish pesticides, find nourishment
by growing crops in healthy, natural ways
to enjoy tastes of pre-chemical days.

We have so much - so we must find a way
to end the suffering in deprived lands.
It's not enough to sympathise and pray
we must make sure the treasury expands
enough to make work light with helping hands.

Wildlife must be protected - free to roam
this heritage we share and must not lose
for every living creature needs a home
with safety from those hunters who abuse
by seeking skins and ivories to use.

We are born free. Each creature has that right
so we must put our world in good repair
for greed has grown into an oversight
and left so many people unaware
what we'd achieve . . . if everyone would *care.*

Joy Saunders

TRUST

Trust who?
Trust your friends
They can be back-stabbers
or spread lies about you
Trust the love of your life
Why? What if they cheat on you?
I can only trust one person
not everyone can manage that
Nothing can hurt more
than being betrayed
Trust only
yourself

Stacey Tully

VISIONS OF PEACE BEHOLD

Across this world,
In ignorance,
And greed is mankind's way;
Material wealth and status;
Is all their cares today.

But we hope for a better world;
In distances' afar;
We will perhaps inhabit,
And some peace,
One day acquire.

Oh look around,
Ye men of waste;
See what you throw away,
And try to make a better world;
For all of us to stay.

In forests once begotten;
of natural growth and trees
For mankind's way of living
Has brought us all displease.

We shall perhaps realise mistakes
A new world re-awake
To natural places everywhere;
Is promised for us now;
And earth reborn to naturalness,
Within it life will flower.

Annie-Christi-Anna

WITH PASSING OF TIME

Getting old can create a few problems
you can get out of step with your brain,
the body may need help and perhaps crutches
while your brain chugs along like a train.

Your subconscious remembers the old days
when you sang long ago in the choir,
yet try to remember the immediate past
then it drifts, like the smoke from a fire.

You may now be bald or an odd shade of grey
and confined to watching the telly,
but your brain well remembers that you were once young
was the time you had fire in your belly.

You go to a room and then ask yourself
why you're there, is it something you seek,
but it's gone from your mind and you retrace your steps
to rekindle your thoughts and feel meek.

Being old and infirm though, does have its points
you can read or just simply look mad,
you can close both your eyes or pretend you are deaf
and escape from some boring young grad.

Yet old age it is sure, is not all that great,
few want you or give you the time,
you're treated the same as an old tattered book
or old furniture covered with grime.

You perhaps do not fire on all pistons these days
and your joints may be crusty and dry,
but your brain has a way to play tricks with our mind,
lets you think you're one hell of a guy.

Leslie Holgate

THE PENNY WHISTLE

Through the busy morning streets still damp with the morning dew,
People rushing about, with so many things to do. No time to stop
No time to listen, no time for pleasantries. Just how fast I can
get from A to B.
So full of their own private lives not bothering about others.
They just get in the way.
Looking down on others, less well-off than them.
How dare they sit in doorways, get off your ass and get a job.
'Spare change Mister?' Get lost you waste of time,
they say with their eyes.
No pity, no compassion, no help from me, I've got a job
you get one too,
'Oh and don't bother me you!'

To sit and watch the faces of people walking past. 'From down
here it's no joke.
No smiles, no good mornings, just stern and staring looks
just as if we are dirt on their shoes.
Looking down on us, but not looking at life with all its strife.
Now the day is passing on, noon has come and gone. Still no smiles
and how are you today.
The city street are filling up, people walking by all shapes and sizes.
All colours and creeds, males and female. Adults and children
still rushing by, turn their heads not looking at you not making contact.
Not a word from most.
Then came the sound of a penny whistle, its haunting sound hanging
on the air.
A lonely figure in a doorway a dog by her side playing slowly as
the drizzle falls.
Not asking for money like others do.
Feet and trouser bottoms soaking wet, no hope of getting dry.
The chill of the day has no pity.
Nor the people walking by, thank you my city you make me cry.

Christopher Bean

MY MEMORY LANE

I'm going today, down 'Memory Lane'
It's a place, with dreams so rare
Happiness never fails.
Nor a doubt, insight oh so rare
Remember, you know the tree we called our own
The paths through the woods, ours alone
Suddenly you passed away.
Sadness still is there within
Time has healed but cannot hide
The love I feel for you inside
As I sing your favourite song
I remember
You were my one and only Dad
The greatest pal I ever had

B Gilman

WAITING FOR THE BUS

They're waiting for the bus.
Will it be long?
And when it comes
will there be one, two, or even three,
of the wretched 83!

Henry Rayner

LIFE IS A GAS

Everything is black
I'm as low as I can sink,
Don't ask me to look back
Just pour another drink.
Life is a gas
Through the bottom of a glass.

The future is bleak
The past is gone,
Of the past I cannot speak
Somehow I must go on.
And life is a gas
Through the bottom of a glass.

The feeling of despair
Drowns all other senses
And those who still care
I will soon dispense with.
But life is a gas
Through the bottom of a glass.

There is no way back
Things move on too fast,
I've taken the wrong track
Cannot forgive the past.
But life is a gas
Through the bottom of a glass.

I know secrets I cannot tell
All chance of reprieve is over,
I've come to hate myself
But only when I'm sober.
So life is a gas
Through the bottom of a glass.

M S Reid

BREATHE

Sitting there, staring as if in a trance,
A submerged memory came bobbing to the surface.
Her eyes appeared to be transfixed at first glance.
The imprinted image projected much sadness.

Entering a dream-like state,
She was about to revisit the scene in her mind.
Her heart started to palpitate
When the tape began to play after a rapid rewind.

Choked by emotion, she remembered the tight grip of her hand.
No words were necessary.
Even at a young age, she was able to understand
The vital qualities offered by the hideous accessory.

Draped delicately around the neck,
The tubing carried its weight in gold.
Miraculously supporting life to spec.
But the fighting spirit grew weary and old.

Unable to overcome the might of infection,
Deathly pale was the colour of complexion.
Years cut short, smoking being the only connection,
Having been engrossed in thought, here ends her recollection.

Sharon Reaper

THE THOUGHT OF NOT BEING IN YOUR WORLD

Go away, leave me alone,
That's my initial reaction to your voice,
To your sexy, sensuous, heart wrenching pitch
To the only safety, the only security I've truly known.

You own me, my heart's yours, always has been,
That's what I can't take,
The knowledge that I belong to you,
That you're my anchor, my rock, my sanity.

How have I reached this confused state?
How have I let you steal all my independence?
The answer's easy, just hate to admit it,
That what my heart feels for you, sure isn't hate.

The intensity of emotion I feel for you scares me,
Each beat of my heart, just echoes your name,
Each image I see, is clouded with your visage,
You're my brace, the only force that steadies me.

Yet I'm so terrified, so very, very scared,
So unwilling to take that final step,
To open my heart, embrace the power you wield over me,
To admit that God, finally my prayers heard.

I love you, you hear that? I love you.
The words scare me senseless, out of my mind,
But, the thought of not being in your world . . .
I'd die, my love, that much is so true.

Patricia Cunningham

GOOD EARTH

This is our world
A farmer working in his fields
Reaping what the good earth yields
The seasons changing as he goes
Hot is summer
Then in winter it snows

This is our world
A factory worker in the mills
A hiker plodding over the hills
An aeroplane flying up on high
Its vapour trailing across the sky.

Roger Brooks

GOT TO

Got to be a certain way
To make everything be OK
Got to give in to the way I feel
Got to pretend certain feelings aren't there
Not real
Got to realise he's not my own
He's him, never mine, I'm all alone
He loves me and that I hope
I'll have to find a way to try and cope
Let him do what he wants to do
If I want our relationship to remain true.

M Barnes

SENIOR CITIZEN

Poor tattered butterfly,
a senior citizen among
young, golden ones,
you still try to ruffle
the flowers in my garden,
reminding me of
my own age.

Marion Schoeberlein

WORK

When you have a job and place of work
You do your duties and do not shirk
Doing things that please
Employment is a job with ease

Earning a wage to pay your way
Going to work every day
A way of life
Then, home to the family and the wife

Shopping perhaps on a Saturday morn
Doing chores with a look of scorn
Things have to be done, it's all routine
Through good times and lean

Monday comes, it's at work and all that
A cup of tea in the canteen and time for a chat
Here comes the foreman, Matt
Carry on chaps, that's enough of that.

Caroline Janney

THE ROW

Just as they were going out
my parents had a row,
Father shouted, Mother cried,
they got on their bike
and went for a ride.

You see they have a tandem
a cycle made for two,
they rode off in silence
and down the road they flew.

The streets were very busy,
as they cycled through the town,
the car in front stopped sharply
almost knocking them down.

Father put his brakes on hard
and with fists raised in the air
he screamed at the driver,
'What do you think you're playing at?
I don't suppose you care!'

Riding down a winding road
Father gave a yell,
'Can't you pedal any faster Mother
we are going up a hill!'

A few miles on Father calmed down,
he turned to give Mother a smile
but to his horror she wasn't behind him,
she had fallen off the bike in town.

Linda Beavis

THE MIRROR

I look in the mirror, what do I see?
A sad old face looking back at me
It grumbles, it sighs, as I look in its eyes
Oh, the misery
Behind the face, I see a place
With colour and laughter to please
The woe, the pain
When my eyes start to strain
That face has blurred
As I uttered a word
Oh, the misery.

Victoria Hewson

DRIVING LESSON

We're driving along in our automobile
My careful wife is behind the wheel
I look at the clock, it says 34
I shout at her 'Can't you do any more?'

She yells at me, 'Of course I can
I'll teach you a lesson you ignorant man
If it's speed you want it's speed you'll see
You'll be sorry for giving out to me.'

I look at the clock, it says 95
I thank the Lord I'm still alive
The wife has really gone too far
For she thinks she's driving a racing car.

I glanced at my wife and I said why
If you don't slow down we're going to die
She slowed down to 40 or less
And I was so happy myself I did bless.

When I got home I knelt down to pray
For I was glad to be alive today
In future no matter how I feel
I'll be nice to the wife when she's
                        behind the wheel.

Dickie Anderson

CHANGE AND DECAY

Age grips my limbs,
Oft causing me to falter in my step.
Weariness, the burden that must be kept.
Yet when I to my nightly couch retire,
It takes but a spell,
To dim my inward fire.
Slumber, insidiously sweeps away,
Every vestige of decay.
Strange mayhap is such change.
I am liberated and free to range.
To meet again long gone friends,
And heigh to old forgotten dens,
To share a tankard of foaming ale,
Or passing away the hours in song,
Listening mayhap to a sprightly tale.
Until, dawn's pull will wrench me back,
To the sad reality, that dreams bring no gains.
And thus alas! I am lumbered once more,
with ages chains.

John Murray

TEENAGE GLORY

Mam, Mam, Mam . . .
If they don't learn the name dad,
They are sure to drive me mad.

A teenage phase,
Moods race in at such a pace,
They think it's the parent who has lost the page,
Only because they have gone into another teenage rage.

What's she looking at?
Tell him mam, he's being a prat!
I'm leaving here when I turn 16,
I can't stand it, you're so horrible and mean.
You just don't understand,
It *has* to be the *Nike* brand.

She wants to dye her hair green and blue,
But what do I know, I don't have a clue.
He wants to drink and go out on dates,
All to be the same as his mates.

We can only do our best,
Guide them well and let them do the rest.
And be there for a cuddle,
If they get into trouble.

See I can mind when I was 16,
And it was me, who thought it was my mother,
Who was horrible and mean.

Shirley Lennon

ALL I WANT IS A FRIEND

I arrive at the school gate
I've tried to be late
I see them coming
There's no point in running

They huddle round in a great big bunch
And then they start to kick and punch
Then they begin to laugh and scream and shout
And the nasty names start flying about

Maybe some day they'll understand for real
The way I really feel
All I want is a friend
And maybe all this will come to an end

Karen McGachy (14)

DON'T CRY FOR ME

My darling, my dearest
What can I say
Though we have parted
I wanted to stay

People were telling us that
We were too young
When we had our children
We proved them wrong

You will never be lonely
They will help you and there
Are the grandchildren too

Carry on with your lives
As if I was there and
When you think of me
Don't shed a tear

Don't mourn for me
I have not gone
Until we are together
Darling be strong.

A Whyte

GOD GAVE ME A SIGN TODAY

God - can not intervene because
he knows the wicked deeds you've seen

I could barely believe my eyes - today
when I saw him stood by your side

it made me cold and shudder inside
knowing all those things you try to hide

long before your attempted suicide
his crimes you can never justify

I could see no sense of shame upon your face
to be seen with him in a public place

As I fought to contain my pain and pride

Knowing he'll make you suffer 'yet' again
he's no shame - but still you play his game

your children you use as an excuse
but what about his long term abuse

how much longer can you live in such sin
all for his sake - 'and a wedding ring?'

Graham Hare

SUBMISSIONS INVITED
SOMETHING FOR EVERYONE

POETRY NOW 2001 - Any subject,
any style, any time.

WOMENSWORDS 2001 - Strictly women,
have your say the female way!

STRONGWORDS 2001 - Warning!
Age restriction, must be between 16-24,
opinionated and have strong views.
(Not for the faint-hearted)

All poems no longer than 30 lines.
Always welcome! No fee!
Cash Prizes to be won!

Mark your envelope (eg *Poetry Now) 2001*
Send to:
Forward Press Ltd
Remus House, Coltsfoot Drive,
Peterborough, PE2 9JX

**OVER £10,000 POETRY PRIZES
TO BE WON!**

Judging will take place in October 2001